Next-Gen Blending

Recipes & Photography
by Natalya Hardan

Published by

⊘ blendjet

Next-Gen Blending

50 Easy & Delicious
BlendJet Recipes

CONTENTS

Enjoy the freedom to create whatever you like
–wherever you are– with these 50 original recipes specially
created for your BlendJet 2 portable blender.

Use them to reinvent your dinner routine. Boost your
workout. Breakfast faster. Or simply create the fuel to feel
good.

Happiness & healthiness are yours for the making,

— The BlendJet Creators

Ryan — John Kathryn Brian

PROUDLY VEGAN (V)

These recipes feature plant-based ingredients,
but you can substitute any milk or sweetener
of your choice.

Enjoy your cordless BlendJet 2 from a mountaintop or your kitchen countertop—it delivers all the benefits of a behemoth blender and food processor on the go.

Make whatever you crave wherever you are

Here's how:

1. Make sure the arrows on the rear of the jar and base are aligned.

2. Add liquid first, then throw in your solids. Don't overfill.

3. Tighten the lid and press the power button to blend for a 20-second cycle, or press it again to stop mid-cycle. Perfect for smoothies, shakes and mixed drinks.

4. To enter Pulse Mode, double-press the power button. Blue lights will flash left to right 3 times & the swirl will stay illuminated while Pulse Mode is active. Press & hold the power button repeatedly to pulse. Pulse Mode will automatically end after 5 seconds of inactivity. Perfect for guacamole, salsa and hummus.

5. Enjoy your blended creation and remember to spin clean after each use with a drop of soap and some warm water.

6. Recharge your BlendJet using the included USB-C cable. You can fully charge your BlendJet with most USB ports in about 1.5 hours.

CHAPTER 1

Smoothie Smitten

BOOST YOUR
HEALTH & IMMUNITY

MIXED BERRY
Smoothie

Ingredients

milk of choice	1 cup
mixed berries, frozen	1 cup
banana, frozen and sliced	1/2
maple syrup, or sweetener of choice	1 Tbsp

Directions

Add all ingredients to the BlendJet.

Blend for 2 cycles.

TOTAL TIME
LESS THAN
5 MINUTES

SERVINGS
1

CHOCOLATE PEANUT BUTTER

Smoothie

Ingredients

milk of choice	1 cup
banana, frozen and sliced	1
peanut butter	1/4 cup
cocoa powder	1/4 cup
maple syrup, or sweetener of choice	1 Tbsp

Directions

Add all ingredients to the BlendJet.

Blend for 1 cycle.

TOTAL TIME
LESS THAN
5 MINUTES

SERVINGS
1

STRAWBERRY
BANANA
Smoothie

Ingredients

milk of choice	1 cup
strawberries, frozen	3/4 cup
banana, frozen and sliced	1/2
oats	1/4 cup
maple syrup, or sweetener of choice	1 Tbsp

Directions

Add all ingredients to the BlendJet.

Blend for 2-4 cycles.

TOTAL TIME   SERVINGS

LESS THAN   1
5 MINUTES

GREEN MACHINE
Smoothie

Ingredients

milk of choice	1 cup
banana, frozen and sliced	1/2
mango, frozen	1/2 cup
spinach, frozen	1/4 cup
kale, frozen	1/4 cup
juice of 1/2 lime	
maple syrup, or sweetener of choice	1 Tbsp

Directions

Add all ingredients to the BlendJet.

Blend for 2-4 cycles.

TOTAL TIME
LESS THAN
5 MINUTES

SERVINGS
1

ORANGE JULIUS

Smoothie

Ingredients

orange juice	1 cup
banana, frozen and sliced	1/2
coconut yogurt, or yogurt of choice	1/2 cup
vanilla extract	1/2 tsp

Directions

Add all ingredients to the BlendJet.

Blend for 1 cycle.

TOTAL TIME
LESS THAN
5 MINUTES

SERVINGS
1

MOCHA
Smoothie

Ingredients

chocolate milk of choice	1 cup
coconut yogurt, or yogurt of choice	1/2 cup
banana, frozen and sliced	1/2
instant coffee	2 Tbsp
maple syrup, or sweetener of choice	1-2 Tbsp

Directions

Add all ingredients to the BlendJet.

Blend for 1 cycle.

TOTAL TIME
LESS THAN
5 MINUTES

SERVINGS
1

TROPICAL
Smoothie

Ingredients

coconut milk, or milk of choice	1 cup
pineapple, frozen	1/4 cup
mango, frozen	1/4 cup
banana, frozen and sliced	1/2

Directions

Add all ingredients to the BlendJet.

Blend for 2 cycles.

TOTAL TIME
LESS THAN
5 MINUTES

SERVINGS
1

BLUEBERRY CHIA
Smoothie

Ingredients

milk of choice	1 cup
blueberries, frozen	1/2 cup
banana, frozen and sliced	1/2
oats	1/4 cup
chia seeds	1 Tbsp
vanilla extract	1/4 tsp
maple syrup, or sweetener of choice	1 Tbsp

Directions

Add all ingredients to the BlendJet.

Blend for 2-4 cycles.

TOTAL TIME
LESS THAN
5 MINUTES

SERVINGS
1

SUNSHINE
Smoothie

Ingredients

orange juice	1 cup
banana, frozen and sliced	1/2
carrots	1/4 cup
mango, frozen	1/4 cup
coconut yogurt, or yogurt of choice	1/4 cup
juice of 1/2 lemon	
cinnamon	1/4 tsp
ginger	1/8 tsp
turmeric	1/8 tsp

Directions

Add all ingredients to the BlendJet.

Blend for 2-4 cycles.

TOTAL TIME
LESS THAN
5 MINUTES

SERVINGS
1

PEANUT BUTTER
BANANA
Smoothie

Ingredients

milk of choice	1 cup
banana, frozen and sliced	1
peanut butter	1/4 cup
oats	1/4 cup
vanilla extract	1/4 tsp
maple syrup, or sweetener of choice	1 Tbsp

Directions

Add all ingredients to the BlendJet.

Blend for 2-4 cycles.

TOTAL TIME
LESS THAN
5 MINUTES

SERVINGS
1

CHAPTER 2

Protein Shakes

POWER YOUR
WORKOUT

blendjet

CHOCOLATE PEANUT BUTTER
Protein Shake

Ingredients

milk of choice	1 cup
banana, frozen and sliced	1/2
chocolate protein powder	1 scoop
peanut butter	2 Tbsp
cocoa powder	1 Tbsp
maple syrup, or sweetener of choice	1 Tbsp

Directions

Add all ingredients to the BlendJet.

Blend for 1-2 cycles.

TOTAL TIME
LESS THAN
5 MINUTES

SERVINGS
1

STRAWBERRIES & CREAM
Protein Shake

Ingredients

milk of choice	1 cup
coconut yogurt, or yogurt of choice	1/4 cup
strawberries, frozen and sliced	1 cup
vanilla protein powder	1 scoop
maple syrup, or sweetener of choice	1 Tbsp

Directions

Add all ingredients to the BlendJet.

Blend for 2 cycles.

TOTAL TIME

LESS THAN
5 MINUTES

SERVINGS

1

BROWNIE BATTER
Protein Shake

Ingredients

milk of choice	1 cup
banana, frozen and sliced	1/2
coconut yogurt, or yogurt of choice	1/4 cup
chocolate protein powder	1 scoop
cocoa powder	1 Tbsp
maple syrup, or sweetener of choice	1 Tbsp
espresso powder, optional (but enhances the chocolate flavor)	1/4 tsp
vanilla extract	1/4 tsp

Directions

Add all ingredients to the BlendJet.

Blend for 1-2 cycles.

TOTAL TIME	SERVINGS
LESS THAN 5 MINUTES	1

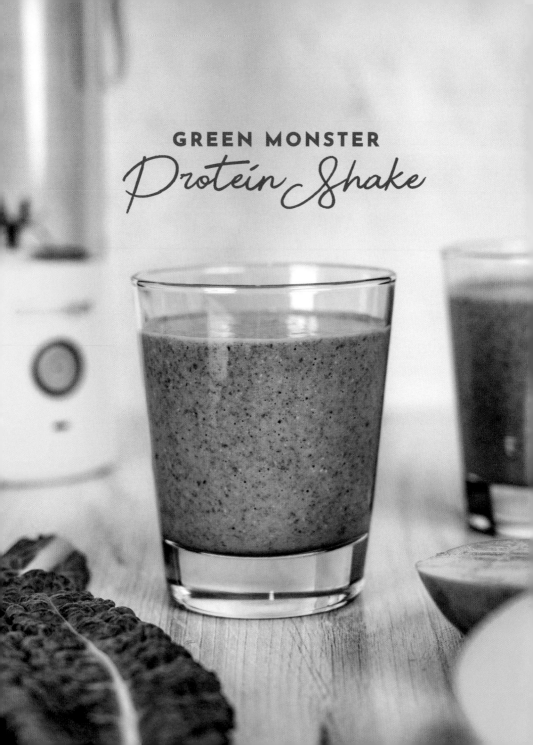

GREEN MONSTER
Protein Shake

Ingredients

milk of choice	1 cup
banana, frozen and sliced	1/4 cup
mango, frozen and chopped	1/4 cup
spinach	1/4 cup
kale	1/4 cup
hemp hearts	1 Tbsp
maple syrup, or sweetener of choice	1 Tbsp
unflavored protein powder	1 scoop

Directions

Add all ingredients to the BlendJet.

Blend for 4 cycles.

TOTAL TIME
LESS THAN
5 MINUTES

SERVINGS
1

VERY BERRY
Protein Shake

Ingredients

milk of choice	1 cup
banana, frozen and sliced	1/2
mixed frozen berries	1 cup
maple syrup, or sweetener of choice	1 Tbsp
vanilla protein powder	1 scoop

Directions

Add all ingredients to the BlendJet.

Blend for 2-3 cycles.

TOTAL TIME

LESS THAN
5 MINUTES

SERVINGS

1

COCONUT MACAROON
Protein Shake

Ingredients

coconut water	1/2 cup
coconut milk, or milk of choice	3/4 cup
coconut yogurt, or yogurt of choice	1/2 cup
coconut shreds	2 Tbsp
vanilla protein powder	1 scoop
agave, or sweetener of choice	1 Tbsp

Directions

Add all ingredients to the BlendJet.

Blend for 3-4 cycles.

TOTAL TIME

LESS THAN
5 MINUTES

SERVINGS

1

PEACH OATMEAL
Protein Shake

Ingredients

milk of choice	1 cup
oats	1/4 cup
coconut yogurt, or yogurt of choice	1/4 cup
peaches, frozen and chopped	3/4 cup
banana, frozen and sliced	1/2
vanilla protein powder	1 scoop
maple syrup, or sweetener of choice	1 Tbsp

Directions

Add all ingredients to the BlendJet.

Blend for 2-4 cycles.

TOTAL TIME
LESS THAN
5 MINUTES

SERVINGS
1

SNICKERDOODLE
Protein Shake

Ingredients

milk of choice	1 1/4 cup
banana, frozen and sliced	1/2
unflavored protein powder	1 scoop
maple syrup	1 Tbsp
cinnamon	1 tsp
vanilla extract	1/4 tsp

Directions

Add all ingredients to the BlendJet.

Blend for 1-2 cycles.

TOTAL TIME

LESS THAN
5 MINUTES

SERVINGS

1

CHERRY ALMOND
Protein Shake

Ingredients

almond milk, or milk of choice	1 cup
coconut yogurt, or yogurt of choice	1/4 cup
banana, frozen and sliced	1/2
cherries, frozen	1 cup
almond extract, optional (but adds a strong almond flavor)	1/8 tsp
vanilla protein powder	1 scoop
maple syrup, or sweetener of choice	1 Tbsp

Directions

Add all ingredients to the BlendJet.

Blend for 1-2 cycles.

TOTAL TIME
LESS THAN
5 MINUTES

SERVINGS
1

COOKIE DOUGH
Protein Shake

Ingredients

milk of choice	1 cup
banana, frozen and sliced	1/2
cashews, unsalted	2/3 cup
coconut yogurt, or yogurt of choice	1/4 cup
vanilla protein powder	1 scoop
hemp hearts	1 Tbsp
maple syrup	1 tsp
chocolate chips, for topping	

Directions

Add all ingredients to the BlendJet.

Blend for 1-2 cycles.

TOTAL TIME
LESS THAN
5 MINUTES

SERVINGS
1

CHAPTER 3

Happy Hour

MAKE THE COCKTAILS
YOU CRAVE

FROZEN
Margarita

Ingredients

tequila	4 oz
lime juice	1/2 cup
triple sec	2 oz
agave, or sweetener of choice	1 Tbsp
ice, float to top	

Directions

Add tequila, lime juice, triple sec, and agave to the BlendJet. Add ice until the liquid floats to the top.

Blend for 1 cycle.

TOTAL TIME
LESS THAN
5 MINUTES

SERVINGS
2

FROZEN
STRAWBERRY
Daiquiri

Ingredients

white rum	3 oz
lime juice	1/4 cup
agave, or sweetener of choice	1 Tbsp
strawberries, frozen and sliced	1/2 cup
ice, float to top	

Directions

Add rum, lime juice, agave, and strawberries to
the BlendJet.
Add ice until the liquid floats to the top.

Blend for 1-2 cycles.

TOTAL TIME
LESS THAN
5 MINUTES

SERVINGS
1 - 2

FROZEN

Piña Colada

Ingredients

white rum	2 oz
pineapple juice	1/2 cup
coconut milk, full fat	1/4 cup
ice, float to top	

Directions

Add rum, pineapple juice, and coconut milk to the BlendJet. Add ice until the liquid floats to the top.

Blend for 1 cycle.

TOTAL TIME

LESS THAN
5 MINUTES

SERVINGS

1

Frosé

Ingredients

rosé wine	1 cup
strawberries, frozen and sliced	1 cup
agave, or sweetener of choice	1 Tbsp
ice, float to top	

Directions

Add rosé wine, strawberries, and agave to the BlendJet. Add ice until the liquid floats to the top.

Blend for 1-2 cycles.

TOTAL TIME

LESS THAN
5 MINUTES

SERVINGS

2

Bloody Mary

Ingredients

tomato juice	1 cup
vodka	3 oz
lemon juice	1/4 cup
celery, chopped	1/2 cup
vegan Worcestershire sauce	1/2 tsp
hot sauce	1/4 tsp
pinch salt	
pinch black pepper	

Directions

Add all ingredients to the BlendJet.

Blend for 1-2 cycles.

TOTAL TIME
LESS THAN
5 MINUTES

SERVINGS
1 - 2

FROZEN
Sangría

Ingredients

red wine	1 cup
orange liqueur	2 Tbsp
lime juice	2 Tbsp
maple syrup, or sweetener of choice	1-2 Tbsp
mixed berries, frozen, float to top	

Directions

Add all ingredients to the BlendJet.

Blend for 1-2 cycles.

TOTAL TIME
LESS THAN
5 MINUTES

SERVINGS
2

FROZEN
Paloma

Ingredients

tequila	2 oz
grapefruit juice	3/4 cup
lime juice	1/4 cup
agave, or sweetener of choice	1 Tbsp
ice, float to top	

Directions

Add tequila, grapefruit juice, lime juice, and agave to the BlendJet. Add ice until the liquid floats to the top.

Blend for 1 cycle.

TOTAL TIME
LESS THAN
5 MINUTES

SERVINGS
1

MOJITO

Slushy

Ingredients

white rum	3 oz
lime juice	1/3 cup
mint leaves	15
agave, or sweetener of choice	1-2 Tbsp
ice, float to top	

Directions

Add rum, lime juice, mint leaves,
and agave to the BlendJet.
Add ice until the liquid floats to the top.

Blend for 1 cycle.

TOTAL TIME   **SERVINGS**

LESS THAN
5 MINUTES   **1 - 2**

CHAPTER 4

Instant Café

TAKE YOUR BARISTA
SKILLS TO GO

BLENDED
Iced Coffee

Ingredients

coffee, cooled	1/2 cup
milk of choice	1/4 cup
maple syrup	2 Tbsp
ice, float to top	
coconut whipped cream, for topping	

Directions

Add coffee, milk, and maple syrup
to the BlendJet.
Add ice until the liquid floats to the top.

Blend for 1 cycle.

Top with coconut whipped cream.

TOTAL TIME
LESS THAN
5 MINUTES

SERVINGS
1

MOCHA *Frappuccino*

Ingredients

espresso	2 shots (2 oz)
milk of choice	1 cup
chocolate syrup, plus more for topping	2 Tbsp
maple syrup, optional *(this will depend on the sweetness of your chocolate syrup)*	1 Tbsp
ice, float to top	
coconut whipped cream, for topping	

Directions

Add espresso, milk, chocolate syrup, and maple syrup to the BlendJet. Add ice until the liquid floats to the top.

Blend for 1 cycle.

Top with coconut whipped cream and chocolate syrup.

TOTAL TIME

LESS THAN
5 MINUTES

SERVINGS

1

BLENDED ICED
Chai Latte

Ingredients

chai tea	1 cup
milk of choice	1/3 cup
maple syrup	1 Tbsp
vanilla extract	1/2 tsp
ice, float to top	
coconut whipped cream, for topping	
cinnamon, for topping	

Directions

Add chai tea, milk, maple syrup, and vanilla to the BlendJet.
Add ice until the liquid floats to the top.

Blend for 1 cycle.

Top with coconut whipped cream and cinnamon.

TOTAL TIME
LESS THAN
5 MINUTES

SERVINGS
1

Spice Latte

Ingredients

espresso	2 shots (2 oz)
milk of choice	1 cup
pumpkin purée	2 Tbsp
maple syrup	1 Tbsp
vanilla extract	1/2 tsp
pumpkin spice	1/4 tsp
ice, float to top	
coconut whipped cream, for topping	
cinnamon, for topping	

Directions

Add espresso, milk, pumpkin purée, maple syrup, vanilla extract, and pumpkin spice to the BlendJet. Add ice until the liquid floats to the top.

Blend for 1 cycle.

Top with coconut whipped cream and cinnamon.

TOTAL TIME
LESS THAN
5 MINUTES

SERVINGS
1

WHITE
Mocha

Ingredients

espresso	2 shots (2 oz)
milk of choice	1 cup
white chocolate syrup of choice	2 Tbsp
ice, float to top	
coconut whipped cream, for topping	
white chocolate, for topping	

Directions

Add espresso, milk, and white chocolate syrup to the BlendJet. Add ice until the liquid floats to the top.

Blend for 1 cycle.

Top with coconut whipped cream and white chocolate.

TOTAL TIME
LESS THAN
5 MINUTES

SERVINGS
1

BLENDED ICED

Caramel Macchiato

Ingredients

espresso	2 shots (2 oz)
milk of choice	1 cup
caramel	1 Tbsp
maple syrup, optional (this will depend on the sweetness of your caramel)	1 Tbsp
vanilla extract	1 tsp
ice, float to top	
coconut whipped cream, for topping	
caramel, for topping	

Directions

Add espresso, milk, caramel, maple syrup, and vanilla to the BlendJet.

Blend for 1 cycle.

Top with coconut whipped cream and caramel.

TOTAL TIME
LESS THAN
5 MINUTES

SERVINGS
1

VANILLA

Frappuccino

Ingredients

espresso	2 shots (2 oz)
milk of choice	1 cup
vanilla ice cream	1/2 cup
maple syrup	1 Tbsp
vanilla extract	1 tsp
ice, float to top	
coconut whipped cream, for topping	

Directions

Add espresso, milk, vanilla ice cream, maple syrup, and
vanilla to the BlendJet.
Add ice until the liquid floats to the top.

Blend for 1 cycle.

Top with coconut whipped cream.

TOTAL TIME   **SERVINGS**

LESS THAN
5 MINUTES   2

CHAPTER 5

Milkshake Mastery

STRAWBERRY
CHEESECAKE
Milkshake

Ingredients

vanilla ice cream of choice	1 cup
milk of choice	1 cup
frozen strawberries, float to top	
coconut whipped cream, for topping	
fresh strawberries, for topping	

Directions

Add all ingredients to the BlendJet.

Blend for 1 -2 cycles.

Top with coconut whipped cream and fresh strawberries.

TOTAL TIME
LESS THAN
5 MINUTES

SERVINGS
1

CHOCOLATE
PEANUT BUTTER
Milkshake

Ingredients

chocolate ice cream	1 cup
chocolate milk of choice	1 cup
peanut butter	1/4 cup
coconut whipped cream, for topping	
chocolate syrup, for topping	
peanuts, for topping	

Directions

Add all ingredients to the BlendJet.

Blend for 1 cycle.

Top with coconut whipped cream, chocolate syrup, and peanuts.

TOTAL TIME
LESS THAN
5 MINUTES

SERVINGS
1

COOKIES & CREAM
Milkshake

Ingredients

vanilla ice cream of choice	1 cup
milk of choice	1 cup
chocolate cream-filled cookies plus more for topping	3
coconut whipped cream, for topping	

Directions

Add all ingredients to the BlendJet.

Blend for 1-2 cycles.

Top with coconut whipped cream and crushed chocolate cream-filled cookies.

TOTAL TIME
LESS THAN
5 MINUTES

SERVINGS
1

SALTED CARAMEL
Milkshake

salted caramel ice cream of choice	1 cup
milk of choice	1 cup
coconut whipped cream, for topping	
caramel, for topping	

Add all ingredients to the BlendJet.

Blend for 1 cycle.

***Top with coconut whipped cream
and caramel.***

TOTAL TIME
LESS THAN
5 MINUTES

SERVINGS
1

BANANA SPLIT
Milkshake

Ingredients

vanilla ice cream of choice	1 cup
milk of choice	1/4 cup
banana, frozen and chopped	1
cocoa powder	2 Tbsp
peanut butter	1 Tbsp
vanilla extract	1/2 tsp
coconut whipped cream, for topping	
chocolate syrup, for topping	

Directions

Add all ingredients to the BlendJet.

Blend for 1 cycle.

Top with coconut whipped cream and caramel.

TOTAL TIME
LESS THAN
5 MINUTES

SERVINGS
1

CINNAMON ROLL

Milkshake

Ingredients

vanilla ice cream of choice	1 cup
milk of choice	1 cup
cinnamon, plus more for topping	1 tsp
coconut whipped cream, for topping	

Directions

Add all ingredients to the BlendJet.

Blend for 1 cycle.

Top with coconut whipped cream and cinnamon.

TOTAL TIME
LESS THAN
5 MINUTES

SERVINGS
1

RED VELVET
Milkshake

Ingredients

vanilla ice cream of choice	1 cup
milk of choice	1 cup
cocoa powder	2 Tbsp
beets (can be cooked or raw)	1/3 cup
coconut whipped cream, for topping	
cocoa nibs, for topping	

Directions

Add all ingredients to the BlendJet.

Blend for 1-3 cycles.

Top with coconut whipped cream and cocoa nibs.

TOTAL TIME
LESS THAN
5 MINUTES

SERVINGS
1

CHAPTER 6

*Perfect Salad
Dressings & Dips*

UPGRADE TO
HOMEMADE

blendjet

BALSAMIC

Vinaigrette

Ingredients

olive oil	3/4 cup
balsamic vinegar	1/4 cup
Dijon mustard	1 Tbsp
garlic clove	1
salt	1/4 tsp
black pepper	1/16 tsp

Directions

Add all ingredients to the BlendJet.

Blend for 1 cycle.

TOTAL TIME
LESS THAN
5 MINUTES

SERVINGS

3 - 4

RANCH
Dressing

Ingredients

coconut milk, full fat	1 cup
cashews	3/4 cup
lemon juice	1/4 cup
parsley	1/4 cup
cloves garlic	2
salt	1/2 tsp
onion powder	1/4 tsp
dill	1/4 tsp
black pepper	1/8 tsp

Directions

Add all ingredients to the BlendJet.

Blend for 2-3 cycles

or until creamy.

TOTAL TIME
LESS THAN
5 MINUTES

SERVINGS
4

CAESAR
Dressing

Ingredients

olive oil	1/4 cup
coconut milk, full fat	1/4 cup
hummus	1/4 cup
lemon juice	2 Tbsp
capers	2 tsp
Dijon mustard	1 tsp
clove garlic	1
salt	1/4 tsp
black pepper	1/16 tsp

Directions

Add all ingredients to the BlendJet.

Blend for 2 cycles

TOTAL TIME
LESS THAN
5 MINUTES

SERVINGS
3

HONEY MUSTARD
Sauce

Ingredients

maple syrup	1/4 cup
plant-based mayonnaise of choice	1/4 cup
yellow mustard	1/4 cup
apple cider vinegar	1 Tbsp
paprika	1/4 tsp
salt	1/4 tsp
black pepper	1/16 tsp

Directions

Add all ingredients to the BlendJet.

Blend for 1 cycle.

TOTAL TIME
LESS THAN
5 MINUTES

SERVINGS
3 - 4

BBQ
Sauce

Ingredients

tomato sauce	1/2 cup
tomato paste	2 Tbsp
maple syrup	3 Tbsp
apple cider vinegar	1 tsp
coconut aminos	1 tsp
Dijon mustard	1 tsp
onion, chopped	1/4 cup
clove garlic	1
paprika	1/4 tsp
salt	1/4 tsp
cayenne pepper	1/8 tsp
black pepper	1/16 tsp

Directions

Add all ingredients to the BlendJet.

Blend for 2 cycles.

TOTAL TIME
LESS THAN
5 MINUTES

SERVINGS
3 - 4

PESTO
Sauce

Ingredients

olive oil	1/3 cup
juice of 1 lemon	
pine nuts	3 Tbsp
cloves garlic	2
salt	1/2 tsp
black pepper	1/16 tsp
basil, filled to top (twice)	

Directions

Add all ingredients *(except basil)* to the BlendJet, and **blend for 1 cycle.** Fill the BlendJet with basil to the top, and **blend for 1 cycle.**

Fill the BlendJet again with basil to the top, and **blend for another cycle.** You may need to use Pulse mode or shake the BlendJet a few times as it's blending to help the basil **blend quickly.**

TOTAL TIME
LESS THAN
5 MINUTES

SERVINGS
2

Guacamole

Ingredients

juice of 2 limes
Hass avocados   2
onion, chopped   1/4
cilantro   2 Tbsp
salt & pepper, to taste

Directions

Add all ingredients to the BlendJet, and **blend for 3-4 cycles,** or until creamy. You may need to use Pulse mode or shake the BlendJet a few times as it's blending to help the avocado **blend quickly.**

TOTAL TIME   **SERVINGS**
LESS THAN   **2**
5 MINUTES

Hummus

Ingredients

water	1/4 cup
juice of 2 lemons	
tahini	1/2 cup
clove garlic	1
salt	1/4 tsp
chickpeas	1 cup

Directions

Add all ingredients *(except chickpeas)* to the BlendJet, and **blend for 1 cycle.** Add chickpeas, and **blend for another 2-3 cycles,** or until creamy. You may need to use Pulse mode or shake the BlendJet a few times as it's blending to help the chickpeas **blend quickly.**

TOTAL TIME	SERVINGS
LESS THAN 5 MINUTES	2

About the Author

Meet BlendJet's official recipe creator **Natalya Hardan**—founder of Healthiir, personal trainer and nutrition specialist. Her plant-based blending recipes use only the best ingredients. Together we're on a mission to make consuming real, whole foods simple, delicious and rewarding.

Visit *blendjet.com/recipes* for our complete recipe collection.

Follow us **@blendjet** for a fresh new recipe each week.

Hardcover: ISBN 978-0-578-79605-5

First hardcover edition November 2020.

Edited by Colleen Johnson
Written by Stephanie Simons
Recipes and Photographs by Natalya Hardan
Layout Designed by Purpura Estudio de Diseño

Printed by Edition One Books in the USA.

BlendJet®
5159 Commercial Circle
Suite B
Concord, CA 94520

www.blendjet.com